MW00875989

UPLEVEL FROM WITHIN

Ten Actions to Boost Your Performance as an Attorney

While Also Improving Your Well-Being & Relationships

Joan-Claire Gilbert, Esq.

Attorney Coach & Trusted Advisor to Law Firm Managing Partners

joanclairecoaching.com

IN APPRECIATION

For the exceptional managing partners and business leaders out there, especially my own clients, who see it as part of their job to nurture their team members to their highest levels of performance, well-being, and leadership ability, in furtherance of their business vision and mission.

He looks for ways he can keep his commitments.

His commitments aren't burdens.

"They are access to freedom and power," says Steve.

"People who understand commitment and live from it produce amazing results."

–Amy Hardison & Alan D. Thompson,

The Ultimate Coach (2021)

TABLE OF CONTENTS

Introduction

Becoming a sustainably top-performing attorney who also enjoys the practice of law takes more than increasing your work ethic or self-discipline. It's about finding a *better way* to **think** and **relate** to yourself, others, and your work itself.

If you are experiencing chronic stress, anxiety, or lowered confidence, consider how shifting your thinking could improve the situation.

If your work product needs to improve, then you need to be focused and clear-headed, with fewer distractions.

If your relationships at work or home are suffering, your empathy for yourself may be the crucial missing piece.

In all of these areas, to experience a lasting improvement, you first need to discover a better way and then to *practice* it continually, until it becomes second nature.

You don't need more information.

You need TRANSFORMATION.

Transformation only happens in the context of sustained ACTION.

In this booklet, I offer ten possibilities for transformation to help you become a top-performing attorney who enjoys the practice of law (and life).

Most involve a fundamental paradigm shift in your thinking and way of being.

When you make an energetic investment in yourself and your ability to perform and feel your best, new possibilities emerge for you, both professionally and personally.

If you are the managing partner or leader in your firm or legal organization, your investment in your associates', partners', or staff's transformation has the real potential to save you a tremendous amount of money lost to employee or member turnover. It can also significantly boost monthly billables and increase the cohesiveness and morale of your team.

As you read this booklet, I invite you to consider what implementing these suggestions could do for your law firm or legal organization.

Most importantly, I invite you to take the suggested actions and observe the difference they make.

These Ten Actions Will Boost Your Performance as an Attorney:

1) Know and own your deeper WHY and your unique strengths.

2) Practice mindfulness throughout the day, even while working.

3) Focus on one thing at a time.

4) Recognize the voice of your inner critic and shift your focus.

5) Focus on gratitude and acknowledge yourself, as a daily practice.

6) Practice deep listening.

7) Stop pleasing and instead focus on serving.

8) Make clear co-created agreements instead of relying on expectations.

9) Be an owner, not a victim.

10) Honor your word.

Action 1

Know and own your deeper WHY and your unique strengths.

Do you know your deeper "why" for what you do? Why are you committed to becoming the best attorney you can be?

You may think that you are committed to becoming the best attorney so you can earn more money, become a partner or shareholder, or gain greater recognition in the legal community. Those are all great reasons to get better at what you do, but what are the deeper reasons?

You want to earn more money, become a partner or shareholder, or gain greater recognition so that you can experience something that matters deeply to you. Discovering what that is can supercharge your ability and desire to improve your performance.

Once you've connected emotionally with your real "why," ask, "What are my biggest character and skill strengths as an attorney? How do these strengths help my firm or my clients?"

When you consciously live from your strengths, you can fully own them as superpowers, creating more confidence, ease, and flow in your professional work.

Exploring your answers to these questions can help drive you forward with a deeper motivation and passion to boost your performance.

Action Steps:

Take 15-20 minutes today to write and reflect on why you want to uplevel your performance as an attorney. Then take it at least a few levels deeper to get at the "why beneath the why." Don't stop until you've truly connected with your heart, that is, when you've gotten below the culturally conditioned "shoulds" that exist at the level of intellect.

Take the free strengths survey at https://www.viacharacter.org/. This test can help you gain clarity as to your top character strengths. By discovering and fully owning them, you are apt to feel even more energized in expressing them, which results in improved performance and fulfillment.

Consciously live from your *why* and strengths this week.

Action 2

Practice mindfulness throughout the day, even while working.

The benefits of mindfulness are numerous, including:

- Increased centeredness and access to your intuition;

- Less reactivity, stress, and anxiety; and

- Improved self-awareness.

Mindfulness activates the region of your brain where the emotions associated with empathy, curiosity, creativity, purpose, and calm, laser-focused action originate.

You can access the benefits of mindfulness to your mind, body, and spirit no matter the circumstances.

One easy way to practice mindfulness is to focus on ONE of your five senses and gently let go of any thoughts that arise. For example, for 30 seconds, focus on the sensation or temperature of the air going in and out through your nose as you breathe (eyes closed can be helpful when you start this practice). Notice how you feel afterward.

Another way you can practice mindfulness is to focus on the sensation of the weight of your body in your chair or of your feet connected with the floor or ground below.

These practices work great if you need to take a quick break to get centered while you are working in your office, but you can also practice mindfulness in a meeting or while you are talking to a client.

You may ask, "How can I practice mindfulness when I need to be attentive to what others are saying?" It is a matter of consciously and intentionally splitting your awareness. Part of your focus is on deeply listening to what the other person is saying. The other part of your focus is on the cadence of their voice or observing their nuanced facial expressions as they speak. You may be surprised at how much of a better listener you are when you do this. You will also feel more calm, focused, and relaxed.

Mindfulness can also help you avoid procrastination, as it creates less resistance to starting tasks you perceive as less pleasant. For important tasks you have been chronically avoiding, first do a longer (10-12 minute) mindfulness session, then ask yourself, "What's the highest value action that I can take right now?"

Action Steps

Take a 1-2 minute break every 30 minutes to 1 hour to slow your breath down and notice the temperature difference of the air going in and out through your nose. At the end of the day, note any improvements in your sense of well-being, productivity, and performance.

Action 3

Focus on one thing at a time.

Extensive research shows that multitasking massively reduces your effectiveness and efficiency. What you did while you were multitasking often has to be corrected or redone in some way. Multitasking also lowers your focus and listening.

As much as possible, avoid the temptation to try to do more than one thing at a time. Close your email, place a do-not-disturb sign on your doorknob, let your assistant know you aren't available for non-urgent matters, or put your phone in airplane mode for a set amount of time as you focus on ONE task.

Find ways to eliminate distractions as much as possible. Focus on the ONE thing that will most move the needle for you.

Action Steps

Write down when you start an important task today and test how long you can go without being interrupted or distracted by a different task or conversation. Do that for several tasks throughout your day and consider ways you can reduce distractions or interruptions.

Action 4

Recognize the voice of your inner critic and shift your focus.

Many high achievers buy into the lie that in order to be successful, ambitious, competitive, or accomplished, they need to be hard on themselves or brutalize themselves with chronic self-judgment or comparison to their peers.

The voice that tells you this lie, sometimes referred to as the "judge" or "inner critic," is also hard on others. Additionally, this inner critic will tell you that you can't be happy until X happens in your professional and personal life.

When we fail to identify our inner critic's voice and set some firm boundaries with it, our confidence and mood take a nosedive. We develop or perpetuate deep insecurities that keep us from taking action toward better performance. We also experience less joy, peace, freedom, and fulfillment.

In order to be firm with your inner critic, you can first slow down to notice when and how often it is speaking to you (see Action 2 about practicing mindfulness for help with this). You can then shift your focus toward feeling empathy for yourself.

After years or decades of chronic self-judgment, many lawyers find it difficult to develop deep self-empathy. But one thing you can do when you notice your inner critic getting noisy is to simply set a firm boundary with it. Gently, but firmly, tell it "no thank you" or "I've found a better way." Then practice some mindfulness, and focus on the good you see in yourself, others, and your situation.

While high performance as an attorney *can* be attained by the PUSH or whip of your inner critic, your *highest* performance is only possible through the PULL of deep love and acknowledgment of yourself. Love feels lighter. Self-judgment and fear of not being enough are draining and even exhausting.

Which do you *choose*?

Action Steps

When your mood dips down at any point in the coming day(s), slow down to observe what you are thinking. Is it a thought that carries negative and critical energy to yourself, to others, or your circumstances? Notice how often this thought occurs for you in the next few days to see how much it is occupying your headspace. Whenever you notice it, take a deep breath, set a gentle yet firm boundary with your inner critic, and focus on something you love about yourself instead.

Action 5

Focus on gratitude and acknowledge yourself, as a daily practice.

A great way to counter the clout of the inner critic (see Action 4 above) is to begin a daily practice of gratitude and self-acknowledgement.

Choosing to regularly focus on what you are grateful for is the best way to be intentional about noticing what is going well, rather than what is wrong or could be improved. This allows for big-picture thinking, helps you access your deepest wisdom, and enormously benefits your performance, well-being, and relationships.

Attorneys (and most people) are often starved for acknowledgment. It can be transformative to realize that we can give ourselves acknowledgement and appreciation. We do not need to wait for others to give it to us.

As an initial step, take an hour on the weekend to fill a legal pad with acknowledgements for yourself and how you have shown up for yourself and others in your personal and professional life. It is a matter of sending "Well done!" energy to yourself. This will create some powerful momentum toward a whole new level of confidence.

Then, choose to acknowledge yourself as a daily practice, not just for external wins, but for ways you have loved and honored yourself in small or big ways throughout the day.

Action Steps

Begin a daily gratitude and self-acknowledgement practice. Get a journal for this express purpose and set aside 10-15 minutes at the end of the day.

Jot down five things you're grateful for – it could be a break that helped you be more relaxed and focused, a kind word from a client or colleague, finding a parking spot, or even just a smile from a stranger.

Next, write down five things you acknowledge yourself for creating today – maybe you put your do-not-disturb sign on your door so you could focus on your brief, you called your mom or a friend, you were fully present for your kids for 5 minutes after school, you made a nice dinner, you stayed off your phone last night so you got a good night's rest, etc.

After a week's practice, notice if you feel more confident about yourself and optimistic about your possibilities for success.

Action 6
Practice deep listening.

In the busyness of your day, it can be difficult to be fully present to others when they are speaking to you. But in doing so, you can learn more and save yourself time while honing an important leadership skill.

As an attorney, you simply must have boundaries with others as to *when* they can speak with you. If not, you will struggle with finding adequate time to focus on your work. However, when you are in conversations or meetings that you schedule or accommodate, deep listening can be a real gamechanger.

We all listen with filters that distract us from what the speaker is truly communicating. We may have judgments of the speaker. We listen while preparing to respond, correct, or advise. We get easily distracted by our own thinking, external distractions, and what we really want to be doing instead. This impairs our ability to be fully present to the totality of what is being communicated.

Listening with filters therefore reduces the effectiveness of communication and our problem-solving ability. Conversations or meetings then take longer or need to be repeated or multiplied. Listening in this way also tends to lessen trust and connection in any relationship.

Instead, practice listening with complete presence and an open mind. When you notice yourself getting distracted by your own thinking or external distractions, gently direct your mind back to listening. Practicing mindfulness while listening (see #2 above) can help tremendously.

Another great way to practice deep listening is to practice slowing down and listening to yourself – to your thinking, and to your emotions. Get curious and observe what you are saying to yourself (is it kind?) and how you are feeling. Be present to YOU. From there, you can then identify unhelpful thinking and more readily bring yourself back to the present moment.

Action Steps

Slow down to notice what you are thinking as someone is speaking to you today. Are you preparing your response as the other person is speaking? Or are you fully present, with no agenda, other than to truly listen and be curious about what is being communicated?

Action 7

Stop pleasing and instead focus on serving.

When our primary focus is to please – to maintain or win the approval of others (partners, colleagues, clients), we are not accessing our greatest power. Instead, we are in a stance of "Am I enough?" We do, avoid, and say things from a stance of being "less than," of needing approval or validation, or of not upsetting others.

For example, you may have some questions about an assignment or project you are working on with a colleague or partner at your firm. Your pleasing self might tell you, "Don't be a bother" or "Don't take too much of her time." Instead, ask if it would serve you, your colleague and your client to ask your questions, brainstorm, or get feedback sooner rather than later. If you wait several days spinning your wheels on a factual or legal issue, you may lose valuable time and energy that could be saved by just having a conversation with your colleague.

A useful question you can ask yourself is, "How can I most powerfully serve my colleague and client while honoring myself and my own needs and goals?" Or, "What would create the greatest impact and be of greatest service?" In doing so, we shift the focus off of ourselves, away from an ego-driven or fear-based being. Instead, we can tap into the power of serving others at the deepest level. We take bolder action without overthinking and we show up as stronger leaders.

Action Steps

Next time you notice yourself concerned with making a good impression or not having yourself look bad, ask yourself, "What would be of greatest service here?" Notice if focusing on this question shifts your energy away from fear, helps you feel lighter and freer, and gives you better guidance as to a wise course of action.

Action 8

Make clear co-created agreements instead of relying on expectations.

Expectations without agreements can be toxic. Just think about the last time someone said to you, "I *expect* you to have this done by X date" or "I *expect* you to do it this way." How did that make you feel? Eager to meet their expectations? Or somewhat resentful?

Most people will find a way to *not* live up to others' expectations. No one likes to feel controlled.

Uncommunicated expectations aren't any better, as they don't give you a firm idea of what the other person wants.

If you hold chronic expectations of others, you either feel neutral when others meet your expectations, or you feel sorely disappointed when the expectations are not met.

An alternative to having expectations is to create agreements. A true agreement is CO-created and creates a space of mutual respect, ownership, and transparent communication.

As an example, a partner might tell an associate, "I need to have this assignment done by Wednesday; will that work for you?" If there is space for a truly co-created agreement, the associate can give a firm yes (creating a clear, mutually agreed-on deadline). If she doesn't feel like that is possible due to her other important assignments, she has the freedom to say so. The partner and associate can then arrive at a solution that works for both of them, without the toxicity and ambiguity of expectations.

Action Steps

Find one area in which you feel frustrated at work and ask yourself if you or others have expectations in that area, which could be better served by a co-created agreement. If so, initiate a conversation about creating an agreement.

Action 9

Be an owner, not a victim.

This is a potentially life-changing distinction that can radically shift your experience of your work (and life).

It's not for the faint of heart.

Where in your professional life are you making the problem "out there" when it would be more useful to see how you have a part in creating it, even if the situation is not your fault?

Did you recoil internally when you just read that?

That's OK.

It's a matter of noticing what is more *useful* and *powerful* (notice I didn't say "easy") – having the problem be "out there" or having the problem be partially or even entirely "in here."

Which gives you the most control and freedom to create what you want:

1. Taking full responsibility for your performance, well-being, and relationships?

OR

2. Giving that power over to other people and to your circumstances?

Remember, this is not a matter of blame or finding fault. It's simply a matter of what is more useful and powerful to create your desired outcomes.

Action Steps

Is there someone at work that irritates you? Do you feel like your life would be easier if he or she weren't around or did things differently?

Make that person your object of meditation for the week. Decide he is your greatest gift and is here to teach you something that will forever impact your life in a positive way (even if you don't see how). Every time you think of him, drop any judgments, send him a silent, heart-felt blessing and be on with your work. Notice after a week if you feel differently or if your relationship has improved.

Action 10

Honor your word.

This has nothing to do with morals and everything to do with a firm operating efficiently and effectively.

When you say you are going to be at a meeting, are you there on time, or are you chronically two minutes late?

When you tell your client you will get back to them in a couple hours, do you tend to get back to them in four hours?

Maybe you fully intend to keep your word but something comes up. As soon as you realize it, do you inform anyone counting on you and clean up any mess that results?

Your credibility, influence, and ability to create powerful results hinge on your integrity – keeping your commitments and honoring your word. When you don't, you and others lose the ability to take your word seriously. Time and energy are wasted. Trust erodes.

In his paper, "Integrity: Without it Nothing Works," Harvard Business School professor Michael Jensen writes, "People tend to view integrity as a virtue that is 'nice to have,' but not as something that is directly related to performance . . . But the increases in performance that are possible by focusing on integrity are huge. I'm not talking about a 10 percent increase in output or productivity – it's more like 100 to 500 percent."

Action Steps

Before you give your word on anything (no matter how seemingly insignificant) this week, fully consider what it will take to keep your word. Before you say "yes," make sure you fully intend to keep your word and will be able to keep it. If you have already said yes and don't intend to keep your word or won't be able to keep it, apologize and clean up with the person who relied on your word. Reflect on how this increases your power, respect, trustworthiness, and ability to lead others effectively.

BONUS TIP

Laugh, smile, and take yourself a little less seriously.

Make sure you incorporate a little bit of play into your day, whatever that looks like for you – a fun hobby, watching something that makes you laugh, having a mini-dance party with your partner or kids after work, or talking with a friend or loved one about something humorous or wonderful.

You will perform your best when you are making time every day to *enjoy* your life.

Action Steps

Don't go to bed until you've had a good belly laugh. You know what makes you laugh – create an opportunity to enjoy the gift of laughter today.

Take Action

Your improved performance as an attorney is on the other side of transformation, which is only achieved through an insight as to a better way coupled with sustained ACTION – *practice*.

I invite you to re-read this booklet from a lens of where you and your team are currently operating, take the action steps, and observe any differences in your performance, well-being, and relationships.

The actions are simple, but they require time, focus, and commitment to become firmly ingrained habits.

Your ability to effectively implement them depends on your ability to see where you are getting in your own way, which is where a trusted coach or advisor can be invaluable.

These suggestions are only a glimpse of possible distinctions and actions that may serve you in reaching your desired performance outcomes as an attorney or firm leader. A coach who is committed to your growth can help you see your blind spots and the exact steps that will be particularly impactful for you.

If you have found any of the suggestions in this booklet helpful, I invite you to reach out to me at <u>uplevel@joanclairecoaching.com</u> and we can schedule a complimentary strategy or coaching call. I will help you develop a powerful plan to arrive at your desired outcomes in your performance, well-being, or relationships, as an individual attorney or for your legal team.

ACTION STEPS

ACTION STEPS

Joseph Hoffer, Managing Partner at Schulman, Lopez, Hoffer & Adelstein, LLP

"Our law firm was struggling with several brilliant associate attorneys who we knew had potential but just could not overcome various performance obstacles. They each had the desire to improve and the ability to do so, but they needed some extra support.

"The challenges we were confronting varied from not getting time entries completed by the deadline, completion of projects in a timely manner for turn-around to partners and clients, to maintaining open communications with partners and clients. We found that each associate had different obstacles interfering with their success, but we quickly determined that our internal tools were not enough.

"It is important to note that each associate had the legal acumen, appropriate demeanor, and desire to improve. Doing the financial math, it made more sense to invest a bit more in each attorney vs. start over on new hires where we would not really know their legal abilities and fit with the firm just based on interviews.

"We found Joan-Claire's skill set and approach to be the perfect fit for our needs. She proposed very fair terms for her engagement and offered flexibility to create a customized approach based on each associate's needs. Our attorneys completed their sessions with Joan-Claire with each reporting a very positive experience, and we then engaged her to continue her work with some of our professional staff. Moreover, each acknowledged and appreciated the firm's investment in their professional well-being.

"The results were consistent: associates with a deeper connection to the law firm, the work, and the clients we serve, a ~15-20% increase in sustained productivity, and better team communications and engagement overall. After experiencing success with Joan-Claire we have continued to use her services for several of our professional staff members and are keeping her on speed dial for any future needs."

These two case studies are anonymous (names changed to protect the coachees' privacy) and are used with the express permission of both the coachee and managing partner (sponsor).

Case Study #1

Coachee: Senior associate Jane with the goal to make partner at a mid-size law firm

What challenges did the managing partner want Joan-Claire to address?

The managing partner at this mid-size law firm hired Joan-Claire to help one of his senior associates, Jane, who was, on average, 20 hours below her monthly billable hour requirements for several months. She was having trouble staying organized and focused, meeting deadlines, keeping partners informed of her progress on assignments, and maintaining composure when she was nervous or put on the spot in hearings and presentations. She suffered from a good deal of anxiety and self-doubt.

Why did the coachee have these challenges?

Jane has ADHD, which made it more difficult to switch tasks, and she was easily distracted by email, calls, etc. She would start a task (while also starting the billable clock) but would get an email, text, or call which would then cause her to lose track of her time on the client task she was already working on. Therefore, she had trouble capturing all of her billable time. Her focus was all over the place.

She suffered from a very harsh inner critic, which constantly berated her for not doing enough and not doing it well enough, but she had very little awareness about how much this was undermining her efforts and how to deal with it.

She had issues with a junior partner who assigned her work and who she felt was uncommunicative. She worked in a hybrid workplace but this particular partner worked in a different office, increasing the communication challenges between them.

Jane also had some personal issues at home that were interfering with her ability to focus at work, and she had a one-hour commute each day that was extremely stressful for her.

Why did the managing partner engage Joan-Claire to help?

The managing partner valued Jane and her work product. She did excellent work, but she was not getting all her billable work accounted for due to her disorganization. Although the managing partner had been giving her constructive feedback for several months, he wasn't seeing much progress. Her supervising partners were complaining about missed deadlines, as well as her "tendency to crumble" when the pressure increased, especially in court appearances, or when she made mistakes.

What was the solution?

Jane worked 1:1 with Joan-Claire for 6 months, or 20 hours total. The bulk of the progress was made in the first 4 months of coaching, but it was helpful for Jane to have Joan-Claire's ongoing support and guidance for some challenging new situations at home and work. Joan-Claire was in regular contact with the managing partner about Jane's progress, while keeping the content of Jane's coaching sessions confidential.

Joan-Claire took Jane through her 7-week research-backed emotional intelligence program, which built a strong foundation for her to develop a deep awareness of unhelpful thinking and how to replace it with helpful thinking, so she could remain calm and access her deepest confidence.

In the second month, Joan-Claire also did 3-4 hours of work with the junior partner with whom Jane had been having communication issues, as well as with the two of them together. On a Zoom call, she helped them learn to acknowledge each other, be vulnerable, and speak straight about how they were feeling about some of their challenges. Joan-Claire also guided them to make an agreement about how they would show up for each other going forward, including a monthly meeting to ensure their issues were addressed sooner rather than later.

What were the results?

Jane went from an average of 120 billable hours per month or lower before coaching with Joan-Claire to an average of 160 per month within a few months.

Joan-Claire helped Jane set boundaries in her work environment and in her thinking, which allowed her to focus on one task at a time. Together they found ways for her to capture more of her time and to enter it promptly.

Jane discovered in her work with Joan-Claire that she tends to judge herself extremely harshly and that it's usually not coming from others as well. Being able to quiet that voice increased her productivity immensely.

With Joan-Claire's guidance, she learned how to drop out of anxious, unhelpful thinking and into her body via "mini-mindfulness reps," which helped her stay calm in any situation and also helped her transition between tasks.

Jane learned how to practice self-empathy, which gave her a deeper ability to empathize with others, at work and at home. She was able to better understand her clients' needs (which they acknowledged her for), and she was also better able to put herself in the partners' shoes, keeping in mind how often they would like to be informed about the status of her work.

She learned to ask for concrete deadlines for work assigned to her by partners and to keep them informed well ahead of time if it seemed she wouldn't be able to meet those deadlines. This avoided a lot of the disappointment that partners had previously had with her turning in work "at the eleventh hour."

Jane practiced acknowledging and appreciating herself and her daily successes, internal and external, small and big. This tremendously increased her confidence and momentum in her career. Partners noticed and shared this with her.

Her presentation skills improved a great deal, and clients acknowledged her for it. She was able to stay calm in the face of challenging situations that previously caused her to crumble internally and lose her composure while presenting or speaking in front of others.

After Joan-Claire helped her track how her stress was reduced and her productivity was the same or better when she worked from home, she successfully advocated for herself an additional work-from-home day.

Jane learned that she can't control other people's actions or reactions so she stopped wasting time and energy worrying so much about what other people think. Instead, she learned to focus on what she can control, which is meeting the commitments and standards she sets for herself, and staying true to her own values and career goals.

What benefits should the firm and this associate see over time because of her work with Joan-Claire?

The firm should expect to bill 480 more billable hours per year, on average, as this one associate went from an average of 120 billable hours per month to an average of 160. If her billing rate were only $200/hr, the firm would expect to see almost $100K in additional revenue per year from this associate alone. Not only does this increase firm revenue, but it helps the associate feel more confident about her contribution to the firm and increases her potential for bonuses and the possibility of her becoming a partner sooner, which was her desired goal.

The firm gets to keep a valuable, talented associate, in whom it has already invested a significant amount of time, energy, and money. It gets to avoid the many costs of finding and training a new associate, who may have similar or more difficult issues with which to contend.

Jane, if she keeps up the practices she learned and the insights she gained working with Joan-Claire, will continue to enjoy increased confidence, improved productivity and organizational skills, and less stress and anxiety. All her relationships will continue to improve.

Her leadership abilities will continue to contribute to the firm through her improved ability to speak straight with her colleagues in furtherance of the firm's mission, to be a team player who listens generously to her colleagues and clients, and to honor her commitments to have high-quality work finished on time while keeping partners and colleagues duly informed.

Coachees: Two non-attorney law firm administrators embroiled in professional conflict

What challenges did the managing partner want Joan-Claire to address?

The managing partner at this mid-size law firm hired Joan-Claire to help a couple of her primary law firm administrators resolve professional conflict that was bleeding into other relationships at work, reducing team productivity and morale. The managing partner had been doing her best to help them work out their conflict on her own, but it was taking up a great deal of her time and energy, and the situation was worsening. Other staff members were complaining that it was interfering with their ability to do their work.

Why did the coachees have this conflict?

The two firm administrators had actually been quite close to each other in the past but recently had been creating stories in their heads about each other that didn't serve either of them. They each felt that the other was trying to undermine them, and they felt threatened professionally by each other.

In addition, each of the coachees had been having significant personal challenges (health and grief-related) in the past 6 months.

Why did the managing partner engage Joan-Claire to help?

Both of the firm administrators had been long-term, loyal employees of the firm and did excellent work. The managing partner had already invested significant amounts of her time for months trying to help the two resolve their conflict, to no avail. Hiring Joan-Claire was an easy solution.

What was the solution?

The firm administrators worked 1:1 and in joint calls with Joan-Claire for 9 weeks, for a total of 25 hours. This mix of 1:1 and joint calls helped each of them do deep work on their own personal challenges through coaching while also resolving their conflict together in a safe, growth-oriented, and vulnerable setting. This mix allowed Joan-Claire to help them decide to honor commitments that would ensure their mutual support of each other and the firm's mission.

Joan-Claire immediately set the context in which they would be working together, including their vision for their professional relationship. She provided each of them with audios about creating relationships and expectations vs. agreements, ensuring their total commitment to the process, and she emphasized the importance of vulnerability and confidentiality.

Joan-Claire brought the two firm administrators through her 7-week research-backed emotional intelligence program together, which built a strong foundation for each of them to develop a deep awareness of unhelpful thinking and how to replace it with helpful thinking.

What were the results?

The two firm administrators went from being each other's professional nemesis to being each other's #1 support person at work (their own words), over the course of a couple of months. The managing partner and other team members were amazed at the shift and extremely pleased with the results.

They each expressed how valuable the coaching and tools they learned were in both their personal and professional lives. Their respective family members commented to them how they seemed amazingly relaxed and focused, despite the challenging personal circumstances they each were experiencing.

Some of the biggest shifts Coachee A shared with Joan-Claire:

1) Increased work productivity with less stress;

2) Awareness of how her top "saboteurs" show up in her daily life and the ability to intercept their negative influence before her mind spirals downward;

3) Ability to find the gift in every situation;

4) Ability to empathize with others' thought processes and show them appreciation;

5) Lowered need to understand why certain decisions are made by the partners ("I'm not the decision-maker");

6) Ability to not take what others do and say personally and not have to fix their problems; and

7) Ability to stay calm when others are given assignments she was previously given and not take it personally

Some of the biggest shifts Coachee B shared with Joan-Claire:

1) Increased work productivity with less stress;

2) Less time wasted trying to make others happy;

3) More in tune with herself physically and emotionally;

4) Ability to take care of herself, without needing the approval of others;

5) Zero conflict experienced with anyone, personally or professionally, and now has the tools to stay calm when triggered;

6) Ability to "listen generously" to understand, rather than to give her own opinion;

7) Increased trust in others and herself; and

8) Increased ability to set healthy boundaries with others at home and at work.

What benefits should the firm and these firm administrators see over time because of their work with Joan-Claire?

The managing partner and other firm members will no longer have to expend significant amounts of their time and energy attending to the conflict these administrators were perpetuating between themselves and spreading among other legal support staff. Instead, they can focus on client matters and the general smooth operation of the firm. The firm also avoids the tremendous expense of hiring one or two new firm administrators to replace these experienced employees, who learned the ins and outs of this particular firm over several years.

The two firm administrators, if they keep up the practices they each learned with Joan-Claire and the insights they gained, will continue to enjoy increased productivity, improved overall well-being, and better relationships. They can use their newly gained relationship skills with everyone they interact with, including clients, colleagues, and family members.

Their new leadership abilities will continue to contribute to the firm through their increased emotional intelligence, including the ability to stay calm in conflict and the ability to empathize with others. They have begun to practice five key commitments: speaking straight with others in furtherance of the firm's mission, acknowledging and appreciating others, being for each other (assuming positive intent), listening generously to each other, and honoring their commitments.

They have become true leaders, examples for all their colleagues to collaborate in the most effective way.

About **Joan-Claire**

Joan-Claire Gilbert is an attorney coach and trusted advisor to managing partners at mid-sized law firms. She helps her clients find a better way of achieving their goals by working at the root level of how they relate to themselves, others, and life. Joan-Claire also guides law firm owners to create collaborative teams that attract and keep top talent while increasing the long-term profitability of the firm.

A formerly practicing attorney from Portland, Oregon, now living in Phoenix, Arizona, Joan-Claire is a graduate of Princeton University (A.B., Economics) and Notre Dame Law School. Before finding a better way and becoming a professional coach, she struggled for years with chronic health issues, stress, anxiety, and feeling like the problem was always "out there."

Joan-Claire enjoys surfing in Hawaii, surf skating in Arizona, and spending quality time with her husband and three kids.

She offers both 1:1 and group coaching, workshops, and presentations for her attorney and law firm clients, via Zoom or in person when possible. She also offers VIP intensives and retreats in Sedona and Hawaii to select clients.

You can learn more about Joan-Claire in the following ways:

Website: joanclairecoaching.com.

LinkedIn: www.linkedin.com/in/joanclairecoaching/

Email her at uplevel@joanclairecoaching.com to schedule a call.

Made in the USA
Las Vegas, NV
19 January 2024

84465675R00026